MW01121837

Copyright © 2014 by Sourcebooks, Inc.
Cover and internal design © 2014 by Sourcebooks, Inc.
Cover design by Rob Melhuish

Sourcebooks and the colophon are registered trademarks of Sourcebooks, Inc.

Originally published in the United Kingdom in 2013 by Summersdale Publishers Ltd.

Published by Sourcebooks, Inc.
P.O. Box 4410, Naperville, Illinois 60567-4410
(630) 961-3900
Fax: (630) 961-2168
www.sourcebooks.com

Printed and bound in China.
LEO 10 9 8 7 6 5 4 3 2 1

TO. . . . .

FROM. . . . .

Gratitude is the **MEMORY** of the heart.

JEAN MASSIEU

Blessed are those who
give without remembering.
And blessed are those who
take without forgetting.

BERNARD MELTZER

NEVER LOOK DOWN

ON ANYBODY **UNLESS** YOU'RE HELPING **HIM UP.**

JESSE JACKSON

ONE CAN PAY

BUT ONE DIES
FOREVER IN DEBT

BACK
THE LOAN OF GOLD,

TO THOSE WHO
ARE KIND.

MALAYAN PROVERB

Each day comes
bearing its own gifts.
Untie the ribbons.

RUTH ANN SCHABACKER

★ ★ ★

SAYING
"THANK YOU"
CREATES LOVE.

★ ★ ★

DAPHNE ROSE KINGMA

Being there at the
moment is everything.

ANONYMOUS

What this world needs is a
NEW KIND OF ARMY
—the army of the kind.

CLEVELAND AMORY

There is no greater loan
than a sympathetic ear.

FRANK TYGER

Wherever there is a
HUMAN BEING,
there is an opportunity
FOR A KINDNESS.

SENECA

The only people with whom you should try to get even are those who have helped you.

JOHN E. SOUTHARD

The greatest gift
is a portion of

THYSELF.

RALPH WALDO EMERSON

If the only prayer you ever say in your entire life is "thank you," it will be enough.

MEISTER ECKHART

A TRUE FRIEND

sees the good in everything, and

BRINGS OUT THE BEST

in the worst of things.

SASHA AZEVEDO

I would maintain that thanks are the highest form of thought, and that gratitude is happiness doubled by wonder.

G. K. CHESTERTON

FRIENDS ARE THOSE → RARE PEOPLE WHO ASK HOW WE ARE AND THEN WAIT TO HEAR THE ANSWER.

ED CUNNINGHAM

A kind word is
like a spring day.

RUSSIAN PROVERB

★ ★ ★

WE ARE ALL TRAVELERS IN
THE WILDERNESS OF THIS
WORLD, AND THE BEST WE
CAN FIND IN OUR TRAVELS IS
AN HONEST FRIEND.

★ ★ ★

ROBERT LOUIS STEVENSON

I WOULD

THANK

BUT FOR YOU MY

YOU FROM THE BOTTOM OF MY HEART,

HEART HAS NO BOTTOM.

ANONYMOUS

Kindness is in our power,
even when fondness is not.

SAMUEL JOHNSON

In prosperity, our friends know us;

IN ADVERSITY,

we know our friends.

JOHN CHURTON COLLINS

You can't live a
perfect day without doing
something for someone
who will never be able
to repay you.

JOHN WOODEN

WHEN I WAS YOUNG,
I admired clever people.
NOW THAT I AM OLD,
I admire kind people.

ABRAHAM JOSHUA HESCHEL

Forget injuries,
never forget
KINDNESSES.
CONFUCIUS

Appreciation is a wonderful thing. It makes what is excellent in others belong to us as well.

VOLTAIRE

How far that little candle
throws his beams!
So shines a good deed
in a naughty world.

WILLIAM SHAKESPEARE,
THE MERCHANT OF VENICE

Kindness, like a
BOOMERANG,
always returns.

ANONYMOUS

Nothing but heaven
itself is better than
a friend who is
really a friend.

PLAUTUS

WE CANNOT DO  GREAT THINGS ON THIS EARTH, ONLY SMALL THINGS WITH GREAT LOVE.

MOTHER TERESA

On that best portion of
a good man's life,
His little, nameless,
unremembered, acts of
kindness and of love.

WILLIAM WORDSWORTH,
"TINTERN ABBEY"

★ ★ ★

THE MOST BEAUTIFUL
DISCOVERY TRUE FRIENDS
MAKE IS THAT THEY CAN
GROW SEPARATELY WITHOUT
GROWING APART.

★ ★ ★

ELISABETH FOLEY

Gratitude is when memory
is stored in the heart
and not in the mind.

LIONEL HAMPTON

A bit of fragrance always

CLINGS TO

the hand that gives roses.

CHINESE PROVERB

A friend knows the song
in my heart and sings it to
me when my memory fails.

DONNA ROBERTS

LIFE IS PARTLY WHAT we make it, and partly **WHAT IT IS MADE BY** the friends we choose.

DR. TEHYI HSIEH

To say thank you is
in recognition of
HUMANITY.

TONI MONT

But Friendship is the breathing rose, with sweets in every fold.

OLIVER WENDELL HOLMES,
"NO TIME LIKE THE OLD TIME"

Kindness is the
greatest wisdom.

ANONYMOUS

Those who bring **SUNSHINE TO THE LIVES** of others cannot keep **IT FROM THEMSELVES.**

J. M. BARRIE

In about the same degree
as you are helpful,
you will be happy.

KARL REILAND

BE TRUE

TO YOUR WORD

AND YOUR WORK
AND YOUR
FRIEND.

**JOHN BOYLE O'REILLY,
"RULES OF THE ROAD"**

THE SINCERE **FRIENDS** OF THIS WORLD ARE AS

SHIP

LIGHTS

IN THE STORMIEST OF NIGHTS.

GIOTTO

God gave you a gift of 86,400 seconds today. Have you used one to say "thank you"?

WILLIAM ARTHUR WARD

THE SMALLEST ACT
OF KINDNESS IS WORTH
MORE THAN THE
GRANDEST INTENTION.

OSCAR WILDE

Hem your blessings with

TH👍NKFULNESS

so they don't unravel.

ANONYMOUS

We can only be said
to be alive in those
moments when our
hearts are conscious
of our treasures.

THORNTON WILDER

No duty is more
urgent than that of
returning thanks.

JAMES ALLEN

Every time we remember
TO SAY "THANK YOU,"
we experience nothing less
THAN HEAVEN ON EARTH.

SARAH BAN BREATHNACH

I awoke this morning
with devout thanksgiving
for my friends, the
old and the new.

RALPH WALDO EMERSON

A thankful heart is
not only the greatest
virtue, but the
parent of all other

VIRTUES.

CICERO

Remember, the greatest gift is not found in a store nor under a tree, but in the hearts of true friends.

CINDY LEW

Gratitude makes sense of **OUR PAST, BRINGS PEACE** for today, and creates a **VISION FOR TOMORROW.**

MELODY BEATTIE

The greatest good you can do for another is not just to share your riches but to reveal to him his own.

BENJAMIN DISRAELI

THE ROOTS OF ALL GOODNESS

LIE IN THE SOIL OF APPRECIATION FOR GOODNESS.

THE DALAI LAMA

Feeling gratitude and not expressing it is like wrapping a present and not giving it.

WILLIAM ARTHUR WARD

★ ★ ★

LET US BE GRATEFUL TO
PEOPLE WHO MAKE US HAPPY;
THEY ARE THE CHARMING
GARDENERS WHO MAKE OUR
SOULS BLOSSOM.

★ ★ ★

MARCEL PROUST

We make a living by what
we get, but we make a
life by what we give.

NORMAN MACEWAN

There is a calmness
TO A LIFE LIVED
in gratitude, a quiet joy.

RALPH H. BLUM

Friendship is always a
sweet responsibility,
never an opportunity.

KAHLIL GIBRAN

HOW BEAUTIFUL
a day can be, when
KINDNESS TOUCHES IT!

GEORGE ELLISTON

BETTER THAN A THOUSAND HOLLOW VERSES

**IS ONE
VERSE
THAT
BRINGS
PEACE.**

GAUTAMA BUDDHA

Verily, great grace may go with a little gift; and precious are all things that come from friends.

THEOCRITUS

A faithful friend is
the medicine of

LIFE.

JESUS BEN SIRACH

What is uttered from the heart alone, will win the hearts of others to your own.

JOHANN WOLFGANG VON GOETHE

There is nothing on **THIS EARTH TO BE** prized more than **TRUE FRIENDSHIP.**

ST. THOMAS AQUINAS

...REMEMBER, WE ALL STUMBLE, EVERY THAT'S WHY IT'S A COMFORT TO GO HAND

ONE OF US.

IN HAND.

EMILY KIMBROUGH

Friendship is a
sheltering tree.

**SAMUEL TAYLOR COLERIDGE,
"YOUTH AND AGE"**

THE BEST ➡ MIRROR IS AN OLD FRIEND.

GEORGE HERBERT

Every gift which is given,
even though it be small,
is in reality great, if it is
given with affection.

PINDAR

SOMETIMES YOU PUT
WALLS UP NOT TO KEEP
PEOPLE OUT, BUT TO SEE
WHO CARES ENOUGH TO
BREAK THEM DOWN.

ANONYMOUS

Gratitude is the fairest
blossom which springs
FROM THE S☺UL;
and the heart of man
knoweth none more fragrant.

HOSEA BALLOU

If you want to
turn your life around,
try thankfulness.
It will change your
life mightily.

GERALD GOOD

WE OFTEN TAKE
for granted the very things
THAT MOST
deserve our gratitude.

CYNTHIA OZICK

It isn't what you have
in your pocket that
makes you thankful,
but what you have
in your heart.

ANONYMOUS

A man's true wealth—is the good that he does in this world to his

FELLOWS.

MUHAMMAD

When you are grateful,
fear disappears and
abundance appears.

TONY ROBBINS

...I felt a glow about my **HEART THAT, IF IT WERE** not indigestion, I think must **HAVE BEEN GRATITUDE...**

BENJAMIN DISRAELI

The gifts that one
receives for giving are
so immeasurable that
it is almost an injustice
to accept them.

ANONYMOUS

I THINK I BEGAN
LEARNING THAT
THOSE WHO ARE
HAPPIEST

ARE THOSE
WHO DO
THE MOST
FOR
OTHERS.

BOOKER T. WASHINGTON

Unselfish and noble actions are the most radiant pages in the biography of souls.

DAVID THOMAS

THOU THAT HAST GIV'N SO MUCH TO ME

GIVE ONE THING MORE, A GRATEFUL HEART.

GEORGE HERBERT, "GRATEFULNESSE"

Silent gratitude isn't
much use to anyone.

GLADYS BROWYN STERN

★ ★ ★

THE THANKFUL RECEIVER
BEARS A PLENTIFUL HARVEST.

★ ★ ★

WILLIAM BLAKE

No act of kindness, no matter

HOW SM*LL,

is ever wasted.

AESOP

Many people will walk in
and out of your life, but
only true friends will leave
footprints in your heart.

ELEANOR ROOSEVELT

I can no other answer
make but thanks,
And thanks, and
ever thanks.

WILLIAM SHAKESPEARE,
TWELFTH NIGHT